D1712553

DISCARD

BECOME A
GRAPHIC DESIGNER

by Tammy Gagne

BrightP◆int Press

San Diego, CA

BrightPoint Press

© 2021 BrightPoint Press
an imprint of ReferencePoint Press, Inc.
Printed in the United States

For more information, contact:
BrightPoint Press
PO Box 27779
San Diego, CA 92198
www.BrightPointPress.com

LIBRARY OF CONGRESS CATALOGING-IN-PUBLICATION DATA

Names: Gagne, Tammy, author.
Title: Become a graphic designer / by Tammy Gagne.
Description: San Diego, CA : ReferencePoint Press, 2021. | Series: Skilled and vocational trades | Includes bibliographical references and index. | Audience: Grades 10-12
Identifiers: LCCN 2020003764 (print) | LCCN 2020003765 (eBook) | ISBN 9781678200107 (hardcover) | ISBN 9781678200114 (eBook)
Subjects: LCSH: Graphic arts--Vocational guidance--Juvenile literature. | Graphic artists--Juvenile literature. | Web site development--Vocational guidance--Juvenile literature.
Classification: LCC NC1001 .G34 2020 (print) | LCC NC1001 (eBook) | DDC 741.6203--dc23
LC record available at https://lccn.loc.gov/2020003764
LC eBook record available at https://lccn.loc.gov/2020003765

CONTENTS

AT A GLANCE

- Graphic designers create a variety of art and other images for companies.

- Almost all businesses have design needs.

- Graphic designers work in several industries. Some work in marketing. Others work in publishing. They may also work in computer systems.

- Some graphic designers work for design companies. Others work in the design departments of bigger companies. Some own their own businesses.

- Many graphic designers have earned a college degree.

- Some design students gain experience through internships or apprenticeships.

- In a typical workday, designers attend meetings. They also work on projects.

- Graphic designers must juggle multiple tasks.

- The graphic design industry is growing in the United States. It is expected that 8,800 jobs will be added between 2018 and 2028.

WHY BECOME A GRAPHIC DESIGNER?

Chip Kidd studied graphic design at Penn State University. But he did not know what type of designer he wanted to be. He applied for many jobs just hoping to get a chance. All he knew was that he wanted to work in New York City. He met with every company that gave

Graphic designers can work on many different types of projects.

him an interview. The first one to offer him

a job was a publishing house. This book

publisher needed graphic designers. The

work involved designing book covers. It did

Graphic designers often learn from others before they do projects on their own.

not sound exciting to Kidd. But it was a job in his favorite city. He said yes right away.

For a while, he did not do any design work. He started as the assistant to the art director. This allowed him to learn how the company worked. He finally started designing covers about six months later.

Kidd was surprised by how much he enjoyed working on books. Readers loved his designs. Soon his work appeared on books by top-selling authors. One of his best-known covers was for *Jurassic Park* by Michael Crichton. Kidd's art was also used when the book was made into a movie series. These accomplishments made him one of the most famous graphic designers in the world.

Kidd learned a lot about the book design business. He loved matching authors' visions for their books. But sometimes people were not happy with his work.

"What I don't like . . . is when you feel that you've done the right work and then it gets rejected," says Kidd.[1] But he also learned that sometimes even the best designers have to deal with **criticism**. Redoing projects is part of the job.

Designing book covers is just one job that graphic designers can have. Other designers work for magazines or advertising agencies. They may work for web design businesses. For these companies, they work in design departments.

Other designers work for graphic design companies. Or sometimes they work

All graphic designers have to face criticism occasionally.

for themselves. These designers have

a wide range of **clients**. Clients could

be individuals or other companies. Each

client's design needs are different. This

gives graphic designers plenty of ways to

apply their skills.

CHAPTER ONE

WHAT DOES A GRAPHIC DESIGNER DO?

Graphic designers help businesses share information with customers. They do this by creating visual concepts. Concepts are ideas. Graphic designers use color and **type** to create their concepts. They also may use illustrations or photographs. Most designers create their

Graphic designers create concepts to show different design ideas.

designs using a computer. All these parts

work together to communicate an idea.

Graphic designers work for a variety

of businesses. Nearly all businesses use

graphic design. One thing any company

needs is an eye-catching logo. This symbol

turns the company's name into artwork.

Customers link this artwork to the company.

A logo is an important part of **marketing**.

It is featured on a company's sign and

website. It appears on business cards

and brochures. Graphic designers create

FREELANCING

Nearly 25 percent of graphic designers in the United States are freelancers. This means that they work for themselves. They take projects from different companies instead of working for just one. Freelancers set their own schedules. They also choose which assignments they want. But they do not get employer benefits. For example, they do not get health insurance or paid vacation time from the companies they work for.

Companies often want a logo to reflect their brand.

logos and other advertising materials for

their clients.

Every business has different graphic

design needs. Shoe stores need sale flyers.

Restaurants need menus. Companies

that make products need packaging.

Designers help create a visual **brand** for

each company. The brand should be

visually pleasing. Designers want to grab the attention of as many customers as possible.

WHAT MAKES A DESIGN PLEASING?

Creating the right design is important. Inviting images help companies make money. Alice Jackson writes about marketing. She explains, "A good design captures the attention of potential customers. It can generate an interest in the product and motivate a customer to purchase it."[2] Customers buy things they find pleasing. Designers can please customers with pretty packaging or a

A good graphic designer can work with many styles.

cool website. Even the way a store looks

can lead customers to buy products.

   Different clients want different things.

Not every job demands high levels of

creativity. Designers must understand this.

Alan Tabish is a graphic designer. He works

with government agencies. He explains,

"Government folks tend to like simple graphics that clearly explain a process."[3] But a day care or a party planner may want lots of colorful images. Businesses like these want to seem fun.

Clients give **feedback** on designs. But not all feedback is positive. Designers may

THE IMPORTANCE OF A PORTFOLIO

All graphic designers should keep a portfolio. This is a collection of their best work. It can be displayed online. Designers may also carry examples of their work to interviews. It is smart to give both options to potential employers. Portfolios may include various stages of projects. Sketches and later steps of a project show a new company how the work developed. Early work can even show a designer's problem-solving skills.

not like the feedback. But they must not

take criticism personally. What matters most

is that the clients are happy with the results.

Graphic designers must adjust the design

if their clients do not like it. Sometimes

this can mean starting over completely.

Designers may even need to do this more

than once. A happy client is worth the extra

work this takes.

THE MANY TYPES OF GRAPHIC DESIGNERS

Many graphic designers work in a specific

field. Some designers work for magazines

or other publishers. They have many roles.

These designers may draw illustrations.

They may lay out text or design covers.

Other designers in publishing create

advertising items such as book catalogs.

Some graphic designers work with web

content. Websites can feature many types

of design. Still images, videos, and cartoons

are common elements. Graphic designers

also create the visual parts of mobile apps.

Nearly every business wants an app that

looks good. It should not only look good.

It must also be easy for customers to use.

Graphic designers must consider this in

their designs.

Graphic designers can use their artistic skills in many different ways.

Some designers work as photo editors.

They choose the best product images to

use on a website or app. These designers

tweak the quality of the images. They use

photo editing computer programs.

GRAPHIC DESIGN SKILLS

Most graphic designers love art. But they may not be good at all types of art. Some designers have amazing drawing abilities. Others have a knack for choosing **fonts** and arranging text. Each of these talents can make a person an effective graphic designer. But designers need more than natural talent.

Graphic designers need many skills to succeed. For example, they need strong communication skills. They must listen to clients. Clients explain what message they want to share with customers. Designers

Graphic designers choose fonts or sometimes create their own.

must then put the message into another

form. This may be a poster, billboard, or

magazine ad. Designers also must explain

their work to clients. Presenting ideas and

getting feedback are big parts of this job.

Computer programs allow designers to edit images.

Graphic designers use several computer programs. A company called Adobe provides many of them. InDesign is one example. It allows designers to create layouts. Designers edit photos and images in Photoshop. Illustrator allows designers to create images. For example, they can create logos. Some designers also know the basics of computer coding. This helps when working with websites and apps. Code is the set of instructions a program follows. HTML and JavaScript are popular coding languages.

Being a graphic designer demands persistence. It requires teamwork. Designers need excellent time management skills. Deadlines are a big part of this job. Designers must be able to juggle more than one task to meet them.

CHAPTER TWO

WHAT TRAINING DO GRAPHIC DESIGNERS NEED?

A young person can start learning design skills in high school. There are many helpful classes they can take. Art history, drawing, and website design all teach students skills they can use as designers. It is important to get good

Taking art classes can help prepare someone to become a graphic designer.

grades in these classes. They can help a

student get into a college design program.

COLLEGE

Many colleges have graphic design

programs. More than 360 schools in the

Most graphic designers have earned some kind of college degree.

United States offer programs approved by

the National Association of Schools of Art

and Design (NASAD). This organization

sets standards for graphic design degrees. Some students go to art school. Others attend a community college or university with a graphic design program. Some schools even have online degree programs.

Some designers have associate's degrees. Many have bachelor's degrees. These grads often find it easier to get a job. Many companies prefer the more complete education a bachelor's program provides. An associate's degree focuses entirely on graphic design. A bachelor's degree is broader. It also teaches general subjects. These subjects include math and English.

A bachelor's degree program is typically four years. That is about twice as long as an associate's degree program. Designers with a bachelor's degree typically earn more.

Students can also take classes in a related field. Many designers have studied business. Designers can meet companies'

DEGREE OR NO DEGREE?

Most graphic designers have had some schooling. But this is not always the case. Some people may find graphic design jobs without a degree. But it can be hard to get hired when a person with more education also applies. Not having a degree can also make it difficult for designers to move up in the field. Most management positions require a college education.

needs better if they understand how business works. Design students can also study marketing. Graphic design is a big part of marketing.

Jessica Suhr owns a graphic design business. She studied architecture in college. She later decided to study graphic design. Today, she uses some of the skills she learned in her architecture classes. She says, "I think that a lot of graphic designers have really interesting ways that they came to be in the field."[4]

Choosing the right school is important. The best schools for graphic design offer a wide range of classes. But no school is right for everyone. Some students know what kind of graphic designer they want to be. They can choose schools with programs that match their interests. For example, a person might want to work in publishing. That person might go to a school that offers a double major in graphic design and English. Others might be interested in magazine design. They can go to schools with strong journalism programs.

INTERNSHIPS

Some students learn best by doing. Internships are a great way to prepare for

Students can get hands-on experience by completing an internship.

a career in graphic design. An internship

is a short-term job for the purpose of

learning. Internships typically last between

ten and fourteen weeks. Many people do internships while they are still in school. Many internships offer pay. But some do not. Some schools help match students with graphic design internships. However, many students apply for internships on their own.

Classes can teach only so much about design work. Internships give students experience. These students have a head start when searching for their first job. Many employers want graphic designers who have worked in the field. Experienced designers often perform better on the job.

Some interns are hired by the company they intern with or by a client of that company.

Students can build connections during internships. Interns meet many different people on the job. Some go on to work full-time for the companies they interned with. Others may work for clients of the company they interned with. Knowing people in the field can be helpful when job hunting.

Jarosław Morawski is a junior graphic designer who began as an intern. He noticed quickly that real jobs were much bigger than his school projects. The work also demanded that he perform new tasks. He had hoped he could do things he was already good at as an intern. For example, he was great at designing posters. But one of the things he had to do was design a website. This was completely new to

him. He worried that these jobs were more

than he could handle. "[The tasks] seemed

frightening at first," he says. But with help

he "got the hang of them and started to

learn very fast."[5]

FINDING A SPECIALTY

There are many types of design jobs. Finding the right fit can take time. Many designers have multiple jobs before they find the right fit. They might start working for a company that designs T-shirts. Once they have more experience, they might apply to another company. This one might design more complex items, such as print ads. Eventually, they will find a specialty they like most. Designers can build experience with that specialty. The more they do this, the better they will become at it.

People who want to become graphic designers should have good teamwork skills.

APPRENTICESHIPS

Some graphic design companies offer

apprenticeships. These are jobs that

teach a trade. Apprenticeships usually

last longer than internships. The company

pays apprentices to work as they learn. Apprentices make less money than experienced graphic designers. But most apprenticeships pay better than internships. Some apprentices attend graphic design school in their off hours. Others have already finished school. A few even get their entire graphic design education on the job. However, this is uncommon.

Typically, design apprentices have already decided to be designers. Unlike interns, they are not exploring different types of jobs. Apprentices are seeking more in-depth training than what interns receive.

Apprentices' training is about specific skills

rather than general experience.

Kristy Tillman is a graphic designer.

She began her career as an apprentice.

The apprenticeship was at a footwear

company. She applied during her last

year of design school. She says, "It was a

yearlong program that allowed newly minted

graduates to gain work experience."[6] Her

apprenticeship helped her grow from a

student to a professional designer.

New and experienced designers all benefit from continual learning.

CHAPTER THREE

WHAT IS LIFE LIKE AS A GRAPHIC DESIGNER?

Most graphic designers start their day with basic tasks. Many tasks have to do with time management. Designers will often take time in the morning to plan the day's workload. Most designers check their email in the morning. Next, they look at their calendar. They see what

A graphic designer's day can look different depending on the number of projects and clients' needs.

projects have looming deadlines. These

projects must be finished before other

assignments. New projects are regularly

added to the schedule.

Many designers work alone as freelancers. They must keep track of their deadlines and meetings on their own.

Designers often work with a team. Some

teams are made of only designers. Others

have team members outside of design,

such as writers. Team members must work

together. For this reason, mornings often include staff meetings. Regular meetings allow everyone to share information. Team members can also ask questions. Different designers work on different parts of a project. One person's job might be laying out photos. Another designer might then create text to go with the images. These steps must be done in a specific order. Communication between the designers is a must.

Freelancers do not have coworkers to check in with. Freelance designers work for themselves. They take on projects from many different companies. However, working for oneself also means working by oneself. Freelancers must perform all the tasks involved in a project.

Mornings are also a common time for meetings with clients. In these meetings, clients and the design team talk about

OPEN FOR BUSINESS

Designers may decide to start their own business. A new business needs several things. The most important thing is clients. Clients usually come from the connections the designer has made. The new business will need a business plan. This plan includes information such as pricing and how expenses will be paid. The new business will need a name and a website. The designer will also need to create goals for the new company.

the direction for a project. Designers may make presentations for clients. The designers present a rough idea of what they are planning. They also show samples of designs. Designers may present several different ideas. Clients choose the idea they like best. Then they set up additional meetings to go over the work as it progresses.

The rest of the day is filled with actual design work. This is what many designers love most. For many, it is why they got into graphic design in the first place. Most of the work takes place at a computer.

Some designers work long hours to get jobs done. They may stay at the office late or take work home.

JUGGLING TASKS

Designers often have more than one project going at once. Each project is at a different stage. Designers usually do a small amount of work on each project every day. For example, they might start by sketching ideas for a new client. Next, they might make changes to an existing project. Another project may get its finishing touches. This approach allows designers to use their time wisely. They can work as

Designers often sketch ideas or create mock-ups before beginning work on a final draft.

they wait for approval to move forward on

other projects.

Jan Solms is a graphic designer.

He creates labels for beverage bottles.

He creates rough drafts. These are

called mock-ups. Mock-ups show clients

his ideas. Sometimes he makes these

samples on a computer. Other times he draws the images by hand. It all depends on the client. "The mock-ups are presented to the client and their feedback and input are taken into consideration," Solms says. "From here we repeat the process until we reach a final design and the labels can be printed."[7]

Many designers try to schedule blocks of their day to focus on their actual designing. It is often easier to be creative without interruptions. But changes to the schedule are common. A last-minute meeting may be needed if changes must be made.

Changes also often come with tight deadlines. Some can even come at the last minute. A graphic designer must be able to shift the plan quickly when necessary.

BEING FLEXIBLE

Graphic designers must be flexible about where they work. Sometimes meetings

MORE THAN ART

Some people think that graphic design is all about art. But graphic designers must know how to do other things. Math skills come in handy. They help when doing layouts. A designer should be able to center text or align photos without a computer's help. Being able to speak in front of an audience is also useful. Designers do this when presenting to clients.

Designers meet with clients early in a project to get feedback.

take place at the office. Designers may

also travel to meet with clients. Or they

may use video or phone conferencing.

This is especially common in a project's

earliest stages. Designers learn quickly that

graphic design is not just about design.

It is also about convincing clients to use

their services.

   Designers must also be flexible when it

comes to others' opinions. Team members

typically offer feedback. These opinions are

an important part of the design process.

A project usually is not done until the entire

team agrees that it is just right. Then the

clients still need to weigh in. They may want

changes. If so, more work lies ahead. When

everyone is happy, the design receives final

approval. The project is complete when

the final design is printed or the website

Many designers like using multiple monitors to see different parts of their projects.

goes live. For many designers, this is the

most exciting point of any project.

TOOLS DESIGNERS USE EVERY DAY

Designers use computers every day.

Sometimes they use laptops. Laptops are

portable. They make it easy to adjust

projects. Designers can do this at meetings or at home. At the office, designers may connect their laptops to larger monitors. Designers prefer large monitors. Some designers use more than one monitor at once. It can be helpful to see multiple parts of a project at the same time.

Modern designers often start projects with hand sketches. They may sketch on paper. But many use tablets. Designers connect these devices to their computers. They use styluses, which look like pens. A stylus draws on a tablet. The drawing shows up on the computer screen.

Some tablets have touch screens. The styluses for these draw directly on the screen. Designers can then edit the image with computer programs. They can add more detail or change the image in all sorts of ways. They can make it bigger or a different color. What begins as a hand-drawn picture can quickly become an animated image. Using technology like this takes much less time than doing all the work by hand.

Many of today's best tools help save time. For example, colors may not look right on a final project. Then designers have

Tablets allow designers to sketch digitally.

to redo their work. Designers avoid this

problem by using color calibrators. These

tools make sure the monitor displays each

color properly.

Having up-to-date technology makes it much easier to share designs with colleagues and clients.

Designers usually spend long hours sitting at computers. Standing desks make work more comfortable. Designers with these desks can avoid back and neck problems. Sitting in one position too long can cause these health problems.

Designers must follow new technology. Design tools are always improving. They help designers quickly finish complex work. Among these tools are laptops, smartphones, and tablets. They make it easy to send and receive images. Jonathan Leahy Maharaj is a graphic designer. He knows the difference technology makes. He saw it during a client meeting. He says, "I was able to send files to my colleague to edit and send back to show the client in that same meeting."[8] He explains that this action was impossible not long ago.

CHAPTER FOUR

WHAT IS THE FUTURE FOR GRAPHIC DESIGNERS?

G raphic design is important for nearly all businesses. Designers can help companies earn more money. Colorful signs, fliers, or coupons can bring in new customers. Graphic design is also good for growing businesses.

Graphic designers are in demand. The industry is expected to grow.

Designers can create packaging for new

products. They can update logos to keep

a brand fresh. The graphic design industry

itself is growing for these reasons. The

US Bureau of Labor Statistics (BLS) projects

job growth. It expects graphic design will likely grow 3 percent overall between 2018 and 2028. This is slower than the average for all jobs. That means that competition for design positions will be high. Successful designers will be those who are on top of trends and technology.

TECHNOLOGY AND DESIGN'S FUTURE

Graphic design is growing in certain industries more than others. One of these industries is computer systems. More and more businesses are online. They need designers for their websites. Graphic designers create websites' layouts.

Improvements to technology will continue to shape the field of graphic design.

They also design any visual elements.

This need for web designs creates more

jobs. These jobs are expected to grow

24 percent between 2018 and 2028.

No one can predict everything graphic designers might do in the future. It all depends on what technologies come along next. Juliette Cezzar is a writer. She discusses the future of design. She explains that designers must combine technology with hard work. They also need curiosity. Designers who do this will be able to solve big problems. She adds that they will also "create new experiences beyond what we can now imagine."[9]

MONEY TO BE MADE

Graphic designers can make a good living. In 2018, their average salary was $54,680.

Average Annual Wage of Graphic Designers

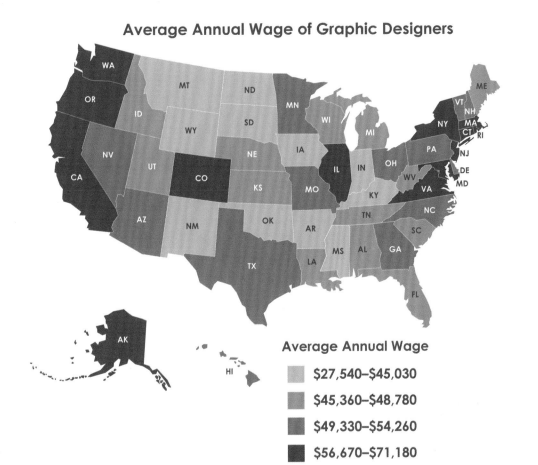

Average Annual Wage

- $27,540–$45,030
- $45,360–$48,780
- $49,330–$54,260
- $56,670–$71,180

US Bureau of Labor Statistics, "Annual Mean Wage of Graphic Designers, by State, May 2018," Occupational Employment Statistics, *May 2018. www.bls.gov.*

This was a bit more than the average salary for all jobs. Designers in certain parts of the United States make more than those working elsewhere. In 2019, the highest-paid graphic designers worked in Washington, DC.

Designers can also design in addition to their main job. This additional work adds to a designer's income. It can also help build new connections. These connections can lead to jobs down the road. Some jobs may even be at companies that pay better.

WHERE TO WORK

Opportunities for graphic designers differ throughout the country. Many companies are in big cities. However, companies everywhere have graphic design needs. Not all opportunities are the same. Certain parts of the country have higher pay for designers. Workers can sometimes find a better-paying job in a different state or city.

Some graphic designers want to work for themselves as freelancers. But this step can take a while. Most designers take a job with a company first. Designers build experience while working for a company. Opening a business is a huge move. Most designers do not want to take this risk until they are sure they are ready. This may be after years of experience.

MOVING UP

Most designers begin as junior designers. Junior designers do smaller design tasks. They may edit images or layouts. Designers work their way up to senior designers.

Designers can work their way up to jobs that have more responsibilities.

They do larger projects. They may work

more with clients. Senior designers also

take on leadership roles. From there, a

designer can rise to art director or creative director. Art directors are in charge of artwork and visual elements. They design the overall style. They also supervise other designers. Creative directors oversee the entire creative process. This means they work with writers and marketers as well as designers. These jobs involve less actual design work. Leaders spend most of their time managing the design work of others.

A promotion is typically based on experience and quality of work. Bosses notice when clients are pleased with a designer's projects. Companies are likely willing to pay more to designers who prove their value. This begins with having the best ideas. Designers must also put in the hard work to make an idea a reality. Valuable designers are team players. They help others succeed. These qualities show a designer is ready to take on more responsibility. Many leaders of design teams began as designers.

Graphic designers are naturally creative. Some use this talent to make themselves stand out from the crowd in a job search. George McCallum did this. He was looking for better freelance jobs. He decided to

film fun videos about getting companies'
attention. He thought this would show
companies how creative and dedicated
he was. He made the videos part of his
résumé. It worked for him. He says, "I got
some good meetings and the chance to

EXPANDING ONE'S SKILL SET

Learning new skills makes any worker more
valuable. Graphic designers are no exception.
They should learn as many different skills as
they can. Then they can find the best jobs.
Designers can learn by taking on a variety
of projects. They may take classes outside
of work. Some designers may even teach
themselves new things. They can read articles
or watch instructional videos. The best
designers never stop learning new things.

show my portfolio to some really exciting people. The exposure raised my profile and got me various freelance projects."[10]

Being a graphic designer can be rewarding. The work designers do helps companies succeed. There are several routes to finding a job in this creative field. And the future will likely include many new ways to apply graphic design skills. As graphic designer Maria Colomy points out, the job is not for everyone. Designers must be creative. But they also need technical skills. On top of that, they need to take criticism and communicate. Colomy says,

Designers can use their talents to serve clients in many ways.

"We do much more than 'make things pretty' or 'sit around and color all day.' We truly give a face to your business."[11]

GLOSSARY

brand

a name, symbol, or general public image of a company

clients

people or companies using the services of another person or company

criticism

comments pointing out what is wrong or not working

feedback

opinions offered by others for the sake of improvement

field

an area of interest or type of work

fonts

sets of type used for text

marketing

the business of promoting a product or service

type

printed letters and numbers

SOURCE NOTES

INTRODUCTION: WHY BECOME A GRAPHIC DESIGNER?

1. Quoted in Spyros Zevelakis, "Beautiful Covers," *Smashing Magazine*, February 20, 2012. www.smashingmagazine.com.

CHAPTER ONE: WHAT DOES A GRAPHIC DESIGNER DO?

2. Alice Jackson, "Top 15 Types of Graphic Designs," *Designhill*, August 27, 2018. www.designhill.com.

3. Quoted in Jenell Talley, "What Does a Graphic Designer Do?" *Mediabistro*, n.d. www.mediabistro.com.

CHAPTER TWO: WHAT TRAINING DO GRAPHIC DESIGNERS NEED?

4. Jessica Suhr, "Why I Became a Graphic Designer," *Perennial Creative Co.*, n.d. https://perennialcreative.co.

5. Jarosław Morawski, "What My Graphic Design Internship Has Taught Me," *Medium*, September 6, 2016. https://medium.com.

6. Quoted in Meg Miller, "6 Top Designers Talk About Their First Jobs," *Fast Company*, July 5, 2017. www.fastcompany.com.

CHAPTER THREE: WHAT IS LIFE LIKE AS A GRAPHIC DESIGNER?

7. Quoted in Tshepang Molisana, "A Day in the Life of a Graphic Designer," *WineLand*, January 1, 2018. www.wineland.co.za.

8. Quoted in Jenny Darmody, "How Has Technology Changed the Career of a Graphic Designer?" *Silicon Republic*, April 3, 2018. www.siliconrepublic.com.

CHAPTER FOUR: WHAT IS THE FUTURE FOR GRAPHIC DESIGNERS?

9. Juliette Cezzar, "The Future of Graphic and Communication Design," *Design Observer*, October 5, 2017. https://designobserver.com.

10. Quoted in Rob Alderson, "The Designer's Guide to Self-Promotion," *Creative Bloq*, October 24, 2016. www.creativebloq.com.

11. Maria Colomy, "Is Graphic Design a Good Career Choice," *ToughNickel*, December 18, 2016. https://toughnickel.com.

FOR FURTHER RESEARCH

BOOKS

Mark Crilley, *The Drawing Lesson: A Graphic Novel That Teaches You How to Draw*. Berkeley, CA: Watson-Guptill Publications, 2016.

Stuart A. Kallen, *Careers If You Like the Creative Arts*. San Diego, CA: ReferencePoint Press, 2020.

Anna Leigh, *Design and Build Your Own Website*. Minneapolis, MN: Lerner Publications, 2018.

INTERNET SOURCES

Deanna deBara, "Design 101: The 8 Graphic Design Basics You Need to Know," *99designs*, 2019. https://99designs.com.

KQED Art School, "Logo Design with Mark Winn," *PBS Learning Media*, 2016. https://pbslearningmedia.org.

Dennis Vilorio, "Careers for People Who Are Creative," *Career Outlook* (blog), US Bureau of Labor Statistics, December 2018. www.bls.gov.

WEBSITES

The Design Kids (TDK)
https://thedesignkids.org

TDK is an organization that connects graphic design students to the design industry.

Graphic Artists Guild
https://graphicartistsguild.org

The Graphic Artists Guild is an organization for creative professionals. It provides resources for those who are and want to be graphic designers.

National Association of Schools of Art and Design (NASAD)
https://nasad.arts-accredit.org

NASAD sets standards for art schools and programs across the country.

INDEX

IMAGE CREDITS

ABOUT THE AUTHOR

Tammy Gagne has written dozens of books for both adults and children. Some of her recent books have been about sports cars and NFL players. She lives in northern New England with her husband, her son, and a menagerie of pets.